NO END IN STRANGENESS

NO END IN STRANGENESS

NEW AND SELECTED POEMS

BRUCE TAYLOR

Cormorant Books

Canada Council   Conseil des Arts    ONTARIO ARTS COUNCIL
for the Arts   du Canada   CONSEIL DES ARTS DE L'ONTARIO

 Canadian   Patrimoine   Canadä
Heritage   canadien

The publisher gratefully acknowledges the support of the Canada Council for the Arts and the Ontario Arts Council for its publishing program. We acknowledge the financial support of the Government of Canada through the Canada Book Fund (CBF) for our publishing activities, and the Government of Ontario through the Ontario Media Development Corporation, an agency of the Ontario Ministry of Culture, and the Ontario Book Publishing Tax Credit Program.

We gratefully acknowledge permission from Véhicule Press (Signal) for the sixteen poems here reprinted from Bruce Taylor's 1998 collection, *Facts*. See Acknowledgements.

LIBRARY AND ARCHIVES CANADA CATALOGUING IN PUBLICATION

Taylor, Bruce, 1960 —
No end in strangeness : new and selected poems / Bruce Taylor.

ISBN 978-1-77086-008-7

1. TITLE.

PS8589.A8816⅓364 2011   C811'.54   C2011-900013-X

Cover design: Angel Guerra/Archetype
Cover photograph: Bruce Taylor. Hydra Viridis from a local pond, shot with a video camera using semi-darkfield technique.
Interior text design: Tannice Goddard, Soul Oasis Networking
Printer: Sunville Printco Inc.

Printed and bound in Canada.

MIX
Paper from
responsible sources
FSC   FSC® C014078
www.fsc.org

CORMORANT BOOKS INC.
215 SPADINA AVENUE, STUDIO 230, TORONTO, ONTARIO, CANADA M5T 2C7
WWW.CORMORANTBOOKS.COM

CONTENTS

The Widening Frazzle: New Poems

Life Throes: Selected Poems

The Widening Frazzle:
New Poems

Nature

The assignment was,
you took some moistened bread
and put it under glass for seven days
and soon a tiny wilderness of mould
would start to grow, as each
of several dots of fuzz
reached out to where it hoped another was.
And all these heedless, headless,
nerveless, needy
greedy intertwingled beings
would compete
to own a piece of food you didn't eat
and turn it into one continuous
thatch of felt,
a little Manitoba in a jar.

That was your "mould garden."
And what it meant,
though this is not the way
our teacher put it, was
that if you ceased to frisk and palpitate
and scoot about
for even seven minutes,
this would be you.
Stand still, and tufts of moss
would fur your thighs
and little plants would cover up your eyes
and where you were,
a soft green pelt
would root and spread and grow.
Which goes, I'm almost sure, to show
that standing still is not
the way to go.

And nature, what is more, is not
a set of laws,

or scenic vistas
or a goaty little god,
but something ravenous
that walks abroad.
A wind-borne pestilence, a thin
old hen that pecks you on the glasses.
Ticks that pick their way
across your skin.
A black squirrel gnawing at the soffits,
desperate to get in.

Little Animals

On bokes for to rede I me delyt.

1

That old book has a million moving parts,
and when you open it to look inside,
they all spill out, like the escapement
from a sproinged clock,
spelling up the life and correspondence
of a Dutch cloth merchant called van Leeuwenhoek.
A regular little factory, this book,
as busy as a Jacquard loom
constructing its bustling world
of high-piled clouds and shambling
courtyards and canals,
and copper gutters filling up with rain,
a 17th-century rain, curled
like a great cascading periwig
over the cankered rooftiles of old Delft.

It has some chickens in it, and a hive of bees
and 16 coffin-bearers and a bowl
(and divers things too numerous to name).
Press your eye against the page
and marvel at the makes that shift
this pretty engine, with its
weights and wormscrews,
tumbling cams and pins,
all shaped by hand & cunningly contrived
to move a miniature Dutchman through his life.

2

He was the first Microscopist,
a worldly man compelled
by wasteful curiosity to build
a homely magnifier and enlarge

inconsequential items: fishscales,
pepper, fly-stings, dandruff, dust,
nose hair, spidersilk, some stuff
he found between his teeth,
and he was the first to do a thing
the finest intellects of Europe never thought of,
which was to look, to simply look,
inside a water drop
at all the thrashing whiptailed swimmers,
motile cogs and quaking ghosts
that make their lives in there,
and these he called his "little animals,"
some appearing in the glass
"as large as your arm" and others,
"as small as the beard hairs of a man
that hath not in a fortnight shaved,"
disporting themselves with merry
convolutions, flexing their numerous
limbs and nimble paws
in a manner pleasing to a haberdasher's eye,
commendatory to the Genius
of their Maker.

3
So, here was a man who looked
at pieces of his world and found
more worlds inside them,
which is the natural order: worlds
that roost in tiny apertures on worlds
where dainty worldlings
dwell, and each one
is a world as well, some
milling in the streets of Delft and others,

pulsing through pondwater.
And each of these should have a book.
And there should be a book
for every punctuation mark
in all those books, and every speck
should be recorded and preserved
so that all things in time might be
made known and magnified
and put before us in the book of books.

But for now there is only this excellent one
by Clifford Dobell to enjoy,
and I have neglected to mention
the best part, which is the bookplate pasted
on its inside cover, ornately framed
in the Art Nouveau style,
and the picture inside it
which hangs in a well-lit stillness,
calm and perplexing as a tarot card,
over a rippling armorial ribbon
bearing a line from Chaucer.

It is a scene from mythical Arcadia, not
the prefecture of modern Greece,
but the literary, made-up place
where idle minds imagine
poetry belongs: sloping pastures
on unpopulated hills,
a billowing meringue of clouds
stitched with careful penstrokes,
a lonely place, at once
intimate and remote, for this
is a *private* wilderness, a place
for nobody to find but me,
and curled up at the bottom
of a vine-laden sycamore sits

a boyish short-horned faun, his hooves
tucked up beneath him, and instead
of scamping through purple freshets,
"trilling joyously on oaten pipe,"
or humping dryads, as it may be,
in a dappled grove,
the little goat is captivated by
a book too small to read the title of,
and look how he holds it, his book,
exactly as I hold mine, his head
a little tilted, one hand propping up his chin,
the picture of perfect absorption,
a picture of life at its best,
because, what else is there to do
in Paradise but loaf beneath a tree,
and dream of other worlds?

4

Or peer for hours and hours,
and more hours adding up to years,
through bits of polished glass
at beings who have no idea
they are being watched?

5

A spring rain pools on the porch chairs
at the group home for addicts,
and the same rain soaks a toddler's sock
that has been lying in my yard all year
and this is the very rain
that fills a frog pond down the road
where I go to collect little animals

to look at in my microscope.
It is all I have done this week.
I am neglecting my life
to spy on theirs! And if I had a shop that sold
button loops and red kersey
and bombazine at 9 stivers an ell,
that shop would surely fail,
with no one there to watch the till,
for you would find me locked upstairs instead
in a rambling sun-stunned room,
the room where Vermeer himself
might well have painted
our hero in his scholar's robe, with his
star globe and dividers
and his cabinet of handmade
brass and silver microscopes, a man
of his time, staring until the light ran out at things
not mentioned in the Bible.

And I am a man of my time, but my
microscope came here from China
in a foam box reeking of solvents,
and the first live thing I saw in it
was a piece of myself, a tiny monster
from the back of my tongue: a macrophage,
whose role in *my* life is to eat
my enemies, the black
jots and whits, the lithe and vibrating
umlauts, hyphens & tildes
that would use me for food —
and that is where you will find Narcissus
today, gazing down at himself
on a clean glass slide,
on which a nano-assassin
encapsulated in a see-through sphere
is taking care of business, and there

in its scintillant middle I could see
my would-be devourers
being devoured, a pleasing sight.
And the next thing I looked at was yogurt.
And then, I walked out to the pond.

6
On the path to the pond
there's a hole, fairly large,
where a pope-faced turtle old enough
to be my grandmother buried her eggs
last year. It is littered with leathery
shells and I have a strong urge
to fill up my pockets with these,
but it is not what I came for. The place
where I gather my samples
reminds me of a ruined Roman
amphitheatre, there are trees all around it
frozen in gestures of theatrical
menace and operatic grief.
A private wilderness, but the air here
is not quiet, it is shrill with sex,
the unceasing, imperious, loud need
of these treefrogs insisting on sex.
There is skim-ice on the water,
still, and there are animals under there, too,
demanding sex, and in truth
I would not refuse it myself,
if some girl with a high forehead
rinsed in the silvery light of old Delft
were to stop pouring milk
or reading her mail
and come out to the musky woods
where a goat-footed stranger is waiting.

But now, I must open a hole in the ice
with my long-handled spoon
and scoop out a helping of murk
to fill my bowl.

7
It is water, the restless stuff
that sustains and dissolves us,
and I tell you, though you will never
believe what I say, it is alive inside,
for there are animals within it
smaller even than the mites
upon the rind of a cheese,
"and their motions in water
are so swift and various,
upwards, downwards, and round about
that it is wonderful to see."
For it is down in the grey
and mazy darkness of the pond
that they are constructing their
glittering clattertrap City of Madness,
with its glass ladders, and lemon-green
spirals and a sky traversed by
delirious weirdos, one
like an angry emoticon, with two long hairs
embrangled on its scalp,
one like a revolving cocklebur,
and another like an animated spill
(as if an accident could live!)
and crescent moons and popeyed gorgons, things
with knives for hands,
frenetic writhers, tumblers, bells
on stalks, a sort of great loose
muscle flinching and contracting,

diatoms like crystalline
canoes serenely gliding
down a coast of brown decay, and suddenly,
what looks to be a throbbing bronze
Victrola trumpet
rocketing around as if it won the war!
And you can almost hear the fanfare
as it plants its small end in a clump of muck
and starts to stretch itself,
and stretch until it is
as long as an alp horn,
as long and quivering as a plume of smoke,
as long and quivering and dreadful as a cyclone funnel,
working the furious hairs of its mouth to suck
its lessers down its throat.

8

I have stared at them all week
in my Chinese microscope and have tried
to absorb what I saw.
I have studied my little animals so closely,
and have memorized their names,
the names they received
from muttonchopped scholars in the age
of tailcoats and columnar hats, there was
lacrymaria olor, tears
of the swan, by which we mean
that it is somewhat tear-shaped, if a tear
should have a long prehensile neck
to wrap around its food,
and there was *stentor* the loudspeaker,
which speaks for itself,
rotaria rotatoria, named
for the whirling cartwheels on its mouth,

suctoria, because it sucks, *amoeba*
because it makes me sick,
digenea because, merciful God,
I have never seen anything like that,
and *paramecium* which slides
like a long grey shadow
through a world it knows by feel,
serene as a basking shark,
and takes what it needs
and gives nothing.

And there is no end to them,
no end in numbers,
and no end in strangeness,
no end to their appetites, and all of it
exactly as van Leeuwenhoek
described it to us all those years ago,
when he, being the first to *look*
became the first to *see*
that what the wise men said was wrong,
what gnaws at our lapsed and sinful
world is not *death* at all,
the old machinework mannequin
swinging his scythe, he is not there.
It is not Death that undresses us,
pulls at the loose threads,
teases our garments apart,
and thrusts itself down
to make more of itself inside us,
nor is it Death
that incises those lines
in our cheeks
and lays his corrupting touch
on a Dutch girl's breast,
or calls up to us
from the cool earth
under the ice-covered pond —

for if you look, simply look,
with your bit of ground glass
you will see what is eating
these holes in the world, what chews
at the black straggle
and clings to those rafts of algae,
and cries up from the pages of a
strange old book, and hangs
in the damp sycamores
hollering for sex, sex, sex,
and probes in the dark muck
with its snakelike head,
if that thing is its head,
then opens its sudden mouth
with its wheel of whirling hairs
and starts to pull one
world after another
into its throat.

Darkfield

Only the scattered light goes on to produce the image, while the directly transmitted light is omitted.
— DARK FIELD MICROSCOPY, *WIKIPEDIA*

You do it by shielding
the beam of your lamp,
and scattering the light
so that your loricates
and flukes and nematodes,
flare up in the velvety darkness,
like hot glass on the blower's pipe.
Your creatures look
as if they were dabbled in glycerin,
sketched with a torch,
or sculpted from drifts of sparkling snow.
They glow.

The moon, too:
it will not show,
unless the sun
is blocked from view.

Except, that isn't true.
Sometimes it's there in broad daylight,
roaming in its nightshirt
like a mental patient.

And anyway, visible or not,
it's always there.

Now we are getting somewhere.

Last summer, drunker than Li Po,
five of us left the party naked
on our hands and knees,
and with no moon to confuse us

and no lamp to show us the road,
we groped through the woods,
intending to jump off the dock,
into the dark.

Then, feeling our way through the trees,
somebody found a luminous fungus
wrinkled and shining like a brain
in the cleft of a rotting oak,
beside the lake.

I must say, we were not difficult
to entertain. In fact, we laughed
like mental patients,
scatterbrains, I'm not sure why.

Shielded from sharp light
and sober thought,
new objects flare
in the night,
things that, visible or not
are always there.

And, drunker than Li Po we lay down
under the stars, newly revealed
on the dark field.

Marbles

Once I had jars of them, a fascinating glut,
and, not knowing our time was short,
I spent whole mornings lifting them up to my eye,
trying to climb inside them, where the swirling
capes and scarves were, shapes unnerving & nonsensical,
a lemony helix, a lick of flame, propellors of begonia petal,
hem of a flamenco skirt, some spearmint leaf,
a vibrant line, a swirl of purplish fumes, and those
that looked like little model planets, streaked
with milky gases, and the ones that were perfectly clear
but so dark you could barely see in, soaked
in a crimson so deep that it damaged your heart.

Having no use but that of being vaguely dreamlike
and awakening a nascent surrealism in the sand
of the schoolyard, still, they were worth someone's trouble
to make and there must have been a factory in Michigan
to mould them, and places that sold them in bags,
but nobody I knew ever bought one, they were just
there to be fought for, gambled or procured in trade
and what one was worth was precisely how much
it was wanted, like art or money, each one a pure
vitrified yearning, a lens through which to enlarge
whatever was scarce and untouchable,
treasure, the future, the body of a girl.

Rebuilding the Guitar

Unable to sleep, you rebuild a guitar in your mind,
the shapely round-shouldered *requinto*
you spent all October constructing.

You find some nicely quartered cedar,
billets of palisander, camphor,
pear, zebrano, bearclaw spruce
and Indonesian rosewood, cool
and oily, heavy in the hand
and smelling of remoteness.

You thin the panels with a toothed plane,
and strike them with your thumb to hear the tone.

You light a fire in an iron pipe
and bend the wood around it, all the while
cocking an ear to sounds that might be in there,
music you would like to hear it play.

Your glue is from the skin of a rabbit,
your polish from the resinous secretions
of the Assamese lac beetle,
you have robbed the world for this,
and these
are the hours of your life in solid form,
the liquid shapelessness of your days
grown into a kind of crystal,
and when it is played,
you can say: I have been intimate
with some small certainty,
a member of truth's ill-sorted family.
Whatever else, there is this.

Then, still unable to sleep,
you come down the stairs in the dark
holding a pillow under your arm,

groping around for the couch,
and someone who does not need to be named
has left your high-strung handmade baby
helpless on the floor,
and what you hear in the dark is
chik, *ktch* and *ktang*.

Lifting your foot
to pull out the slivers
you have to think, what
can be salvaged from this?
So, inevitably, you search through the wreckage
looking for poetry.

Checks in the Horn Timber,
and a Hogged Sheer

What the would-be
boat-restorer bought
for half the value of its wood,
was an unused future,
which had stood
for five years
in a quiet spot
behind the builder's widow's
house;
          and what he got,
apart from a pretty good trailer,
was a new supply
of fresh, unsampled days,
and also the builder's
hope that, by and by,
he would be loading up
the thing he'd made
and sailing it away
to where the sky
is interleaved with orange
like a mixed drink,
and happiness arrives in waves
of salt and fronds
and green volcanos wafting
in a horizontal haze.

That's what the builder thought.
But what he ended up with
was a brownish spot
that never went away,
and there is his Fiji,
flush with rot
in the long grass,

seedy with dreams,
the sun's heat slowly
opening her seams.

Meanwhile, the buyer
has a nautical
vocabulary to acquire,
a trampled field
to learn it in,
a patch of well-packed dust
on which to pour his liquid hours,
and make his own damned
ocean, if he must.

Echocardiogram

Heart, at last we meet.
Fifty years I've held you
like a restless infant in my shirt,
an anxious father
(though we were born together),
and now you're blurred, but there:
shifting like a patch
of scary weather on a screen,
your granular darkness scarred
with light, and beating (I can tell)
too hard, as if aware
of being watched,
like a furtive animal, or
a looter on surveillance camera,
smashing up the store.

And there are the famous chambers,
ventricles and veins,
sectioned like a roman town,
fossa ovalis, infundibulum,
and over here, the doctor says —
and now he is pointing with two fingers,
and speaking
very quietly, and the room
is really *very* dark —
"*une fuite mitrale,*" a bad place
where the valve
is weak and blood goes where it shouldn't,
and I can see it open
and close, and open,
pleading like a fish's mouth.

The doctor of my heart
is Persian and would like to know
have I read the Rubaiyat?
In fact I have,

but neither of us
can recite any verses,
there in the intimacy of our darkness,
and we revert to silence
while he does his work,
pushing the wand
under my sternum till it hurts,
recording dimensions on the scope.

And you, poor patient heart,
what worldly hope
have I set you on?
My doctor shifts his hand, and you are gone
without a trace,
lost in a whirl of ash,

my good heart with its small bad place.
Vanished, you could say, like Snow,
upon the Desert's dusty Face.

Definitely Not

We had a feeling you would place this call
to 1-900-PSYCHIC. Thank you for your trust.
A poorly paid clairvoyant will be with you soon.
In the meantime, please enjoy
this complimentary
oracular pronouncement: You are not
going to live forever.
Definitely not.

Your time on earth is small,
while the national debt is enormous,
and the news will never arrive at its end.
And obviously it is very wrong to spend
the part of you that's left
rereading the story of a long-haired girl
who meets a lonely man in Mandalay.
That book is foolish.
Put the book away.

And it is a mistake to play that tune again,
the one about the guy
whose only heart went gurgling down the drain
in the men's room of the International House of Pancakes,
and now his life is awful and his days are long.
Turn off that song.

And it is too late
to improve the appearance of your head
through the science of Cranial Tectonics.
Time will guide you to your proper shape
and bring you all you need to know.
Tune out that show.

Put down the lip gloss,
quench the pulsing screens.

Break up the congas, toss
the limited edition figurines.

And when the intense young man comes to your door
to tell you what the universe is for,
and who constructed it
and who is coming soon, without a doubt,
to smash it up again,
accept the pamphlets, thank the man,
and throw him out.

But the door itself, you ought to leave that open.
Let the wind come in to live with you.
And get to know your world. It's all you've got.
Cool your forehead on a frozen chicken.
Probe the topsoil, warm with rot,
jiggle the meat that covers up your arm.
You are no better, and no other, than the sum
of all your choices.

As for the rest,
the disembodied voices,
and the moving pictures
and the overtures that travel in the air
these things are all too sad
for anyone
to bear.

Deep in the landfill
there are instamatic cameras
with your face inside them smiling.

Deep in the books
are words that made you cry.

And down in the muddled warmth of your TV

incipient lives are struggling to be,
and failing.
You at least have pulled that off.
For how much longer? We shall see.
Thank you again for choosing us.
Your first two minutes here are free.

The Waterfall

Here the river, in a rage
of fury and self-hate,
annihilates itself.
It tears itself to pieces like a page,
and leaps from its own rocks,
a thousand times a day.
Then, in the smash and mist,
it shudders up again
to hang there like a fist,
shivering with self-disgust,
impatient to be done
and failing, as it must.

It roars like something in a cage,
scraping the walls with its nails.
Even as I lie not-sleeping
in my tent, it pounds and chafes,
milling itself to a fine rain.
Yet in the morning it is there again,
tall as a pinetree
but weaker than pipesmoke,
and always producing that roar,
a sound like everyone alive
talking at once.

I have come a long way
to watch this water fail.
I have paddled down rapids,
through keepers and sweepers
and carried my boat on my head.
I have punched through waves,
walked around logjams
and peeled out from the oil-black calm
into the rushing hydraulics
of the main channel
where the dark water flexes

and slides right under itself.
I came without capsizing once
to the place where the river
spends what it has in one throw,
and my plan is to stay for a while
with a plume of hysteria
rising inside me, as spray
cools my cheeks and my shirt
becomes drenched and just stare
at this collapse that lasts all day,
this demolition dangling in the air
as if caught in a tape loop.
And I can't tell if those are
fluted columns or long white hair
or whether this thing is strong
or effete, steadfast
or fleet. It slides
but abides, sways
but stays. One moment it is trembling
like an Edwardian maiden in her filmy dress,
pressing the back of her hand to her head,
and the next it's as stable as marble,
older than letters,
stiff as the bones in my arm

and standing before it
with shame and self-love
plunging and recirculating
inside me, I can't seem to tell
if this is a wise thing
or a foolish one, a teacher
or an idiot child,
a beginning or an end.

Left Behind

The wooden church (which later burned)
had a padlock on a chain and signs that warned
it would not be forgiving those
who trespassed against it. Well.
There it stood at the far end of our road
in a damp and bosomy luxuriance
of lilacs and feral roses,
shedding those long curls of paint
in the wild oats and chicory,
squinting down at the street hockey
with a certain impotent bitterness,
its eyeslots narrowed under the pointed hat
and the doorway like a mad mouth
in a pilgrim's head, a prim,
cross face stuck in an eternal yell,
warning the pliant fools
and the obstinate dunderheads away from
the place that isn't heaven, and
it called out to me one weekend
afternoon, in the heat of July,
in a haze of cicadas,
and urged me to pry off the plywood
over its chancel window and climb in
to see what kind of glory
had been boarded up in there.

And I think, for the purpose of this story,
I will say it was a Sunday,
and inside it was
airless and hot and weirdly still,
as quiet, you could say,
as a church,
with the light leaking in sideways, as it will,
through the old, bad wall
and there too, as I recall,

a layer of bird dung on the balustrades
and chunks of plaster in the aisles,
and the usual dust in which the daylight was suspended
and the usual sense that time itself had ended,
and that the *time foretold* had finally come,
and gone, and left me there
in that ecstasy of aloneness,
to pull a rain-damaged hymnbook
from a wall rack, and breathe
the old-house smell
and make up a short prayer
to my new god
of abandonment and neglect.

Dead Metaphor

I've spent all afternoon in a well-swept attic
(by which I mean I have spent my whole life in myself)
looking for signs of a walled-up door,
or a loose plank under which an old letter is hidden
(by which I mean I must have more)
and I have gone through the books,
reading only the pencil notes in the margins
and I have sniffed the clothes for a whiff of perfume
and picked up a parlour guitar with no strings and pretended to play it
and at last I have to concede
these things will never be more than what they are
the stuff will not be anything but stuff
(by which I mean that this is either
sufficient, for my purposes, or not enough).

Timon's Epitaph

Timon the Hater lies right here, so move along.
Curse me, if you wish, but move along.

Or dig, if you have to, I did once
and struck a pot of treasure with my spade.
Perhaps I have it with me now!

You may well find a dented kettle
filled to bursting with a soft and useful metal.
So, why not dig, and see how I was paid
for all my diligence and thrift?
Look where my best-laid plans were laid,
and see exactly
what the self-made man has made.

Clock Solitaire

My grandmother once had a house
full of fabulous clutter, the things
you pick up as you go, kickshaws
and sun-catchers, stuff.
A clockwork Scotsman in a
whiskey bottle, bells,
balls, and bowls, a company
of eentsy chinamen with ivory pails.
And, on a big round puzzle table,
under the hemp skirt of a hula-dancing lamp,
a lucite cube with forty dollars
floating in it, real money
paralyzed inside the dream
of its worth, and it was at that table
that I learned to play the kind of solitaire
where you place your cards
face down in the pattern of a clock,
and turn them over one by one,
transferring each to a position
corresponding to its rank, so that
the twos come to roost at two,
the queens at noon, the purpose being
to reverse the shuffle, turn back
the clock, you could say. And why
that's a good way to use up your time
is worth asking, I guess,
but the method is the usual one
of foxing out confusion and misrule
with simple protocols
while praying for a favourable end.
But almost every time you play,
there is already something in the cards
that makes it fail, and nothing
anyone might do (within the rules) can turn

incurious fortune
from its course. The cards
fall where they fall, and if it all
ends well it is only because it was secretly
perfect in the first place.
And so we turn up the hours
one after another, with their
shortfalls and windfalls, revealing
their place in the (apt phrase!) chain
of events and force them to show
what they, therefore, are there for.

And now, it so happens,
the house has been sold
and she lives in a sort of hospital
with her four boxes stowed under the bed.
And there has been some talk of going through them,
sorting her last things into a last box,
because the less clutter the better
and one box is tidier than more,
and I wonder, does she think
as she lies there,
blind and too dizzy to stand,
that she has won, or lost, or that the game
was a waste of her time?

You Know?

Then the sufferer said, give me a thing made out of words
that will make my grief smaller,

and I said, I will try. So I wrote about
the names of paints,
Pompeian blue, pompadour green
beryl, benzoazurine,

but it was so quiet I could actually hear
hammers falling inside in my wristwatch

and I could not remember why I thought this could be done.

Then the sufferer asked for something
to remind him of earlier years

and I wrote about a marrow bone
cut on a butcher's bandsaw,
porous as sponge, with millions of
hard small rooms for the blood to be born in.
Dead bone, live cells. You know?

But he didn't,
and neither do I.

Then the sufferer asked me to say
what it all comes down to

and this time I offered him money.
I offered to fill his water glass
and change his dressings.
I offered to lie in his clothes for a day,

and he said it is I
who am comforting you.

Pacific Coho

In the movie of this poem there are giant ants
and corpses coming back to life,
a toothsome temptress in transparent pants,
a murky pool, a murdered wife,
some DNA adhering to a knife,
reprisals, ribaldry, romance,
a man on fire who leaps from moving trains,
a temperamental ape with human brains,
a lusty butler, a licentious maid —

but in the original poem, I'm afraid
there is only
a smooth grey rock.

And at the film's finale there's a flood
that puts an end to seven years of drought,
So, one by one the villagers come out
and cleave to one another in the mud.
A glad cacophony of kettle drums
acclaims the rainbow, when at last it comes,
and now it looks like time to kiss the girl —

but in the poem
there is just a squirrel
with a long thin pinecone
in his mouth.

The movie has an angry child of nine
who will not lift his eyes or answer
when they ask him if he's ever heard of "cancer."
And when they tell him everything is fine,
that all he needs is needles in his spine,
and probes and pills and he'll be good as new
he knows already that it isn't true.
And weeping in the dark, we know it too.
But still, they squabble on, all three,

the distant mother and the brooding Dad
oblivious to what they have, or had,
until it dies, when all at once they see
that suffering has somehow set them free
or made them whole —

the poem
has a red ceramic bowl,
a parallelogram of sunlight
and a hammering sound
from somewhere down the road.

In the film the writer pawns his coat
to buy a can of salmon for his cat.
He climbs the stairs to his unheated flat,
and ties a flowered sheet around his throat.
But as he teeters on the kitchen chair
he glances at the mail, and what is there?
a late reprieve, a laudatory note,
a handsome cheque for something that he wrote!
The sun comes out, his worries are effaced —

the poem, though,
on which the film was based,
has cold air
coming through the mail slot,
branches shifting
in a small tense wind.
The cat is sort of
overwrought, the man
is staring at the label on the can.

Getting Started

Good morning. In the news today,
some people you may have heard about are dead
and portions of the planet are at war;
also, your right arm is kind of sore
and what's the point of getting out of bed?
Reports confirm that something large and red
has risen in the middle of the sky.
A genius will be on to tell us why.
But first, how long do you intend to lie
snoring in that heap of flannelette?
Get up, get dressed and get what you can get.
It isn't every day that you're alive.
The keys are on the fridge. Get out and drive.

The night, the mothy night
has come and gone.
Your life is where you left it. Put it on
and walk around in it awhile. At first it feels
like someone else's, and it has a smell
that, in a bottle, wouldn't sell.
And yet, it's yours, it's definitely yours.
Now shouldn't you get busy with your chores?
I believe you have some grubbing-around to do,
Some sponging-out, some walking-on-all-fours —
Things that you had better not postpone.
You might begin by waxing up the phone
or putting all your hot dogs in a row
or plotting a Projected Earnings Chart.
Whatever it is, I'm sure you'd better start.

Unless, that is, your job is Art,
in which case please go back to sleep
and dream of food and sex at our expense.
Get up at noon, or later, and dispense
some yellow paint, or weld some pipes together
or think up metaphors about the weather.

You'll be rewarded for the time you sold.
Poet, we'd be pleased to meet your rent
and fill your velvet pantaloons with gold
and froth your mug, and heap your plate with feed
provided you will keep our schools provisioned
with all the strophes and anapests they need.

Philosophers and theologians too,
we'll pay you well to pester us with questions —
catalogues of quandaries you've compiled —
Does love facilitate digestion?
If you were starving would you eat your child?
But do not hurry. The rest of us are slaving,
slaving in the mills and malls
so you can sip the manna as it falls
and make us better with your saintly raving.

As for you others, it's time to start behaving
like Information Officers and Third Trombone,
and salesmen, psychotherapists and thieves,
retailing products nobody should own
by saying things that nobody believes,
to service our absurd, collective yearning
to keep these engines of enchantment turning,
mile on clattering mile on awful mile.
It can't be stopped, so what the heck.
Seize the day and wring its skinny neck
and toss it with the others on the pile.

Our Things

1

Our things understand us too well.
A knife knows my deep
need to stab.
Keys know what I have to hide.

A window sees that I am never satisfied.
How wise in my ways
they are! The walls
remember what goes on
when no one is around.
A thumb piano knows
my favourite sound.

A pen can tell you
what I meant to say,
and who I meant to say it to and
there up high
on its shelf beside the door
sits the crouched and vaguely brain-shaped
bicycle helmet
thinking the only thought it has,
a sordid fantasy concerning asphalt,
bone and what it thinks it knows about
my secret wish.

2

Our things have wishes of their own
which I can read, when I try.
My shoes feel tenderly
toward my feet.
My roof would like me to be dry.
My watch, for its part,

will not lie.
It sees through my excuses,
and, when I shower,
reposes on the toilet cover
counting the day's failures
in faint clicks.
Abject object, made
of lateness, why
not simply let it die?

Give me a minute to consider.
But for now, a sweater
wants to tell me about
the love that made it with a million
little knots,
and how, when hope hurts me
like a phantom limb,
it will let me use its loose
and empty arms
to hold children with,
the ones I have made,
or am making,
with a million little knots.

3

Back to the watch, though, my
fastidious mustachioed
little advisor,
why did I let it
ride my wrist all day,
picking holes
in the morning,
nibbling time by crumbs?
Prim depreciator,

with its soft *tsk tsk*
close to my ear
in the anxious night,
I could pull out its works
and let it tell one time
forever, but it is only
as it was made,
a hole in the air
through which the worries
climb as they are transformed
into sorrows,
noiseless, featureless,
incapable of harm.

Stuffing

One day the new couch came, with its folding mattress.
How well it carried our guests, that little raft,
and how we loved to see their mussed hair in the morning
and their sharp-kneed children, sprawling in flannel.

Now here it is suddenly, stuffed with old dust,
fingernail parings and popcorn, taking up space,
and here am I to pry all that apart
and battle it down to a size
the garbage men will take.

After years of reminding the young ones never
to draw on it in pen, or lose their food inside its folds,
I have slashed up its slipcover, snicker snack,
with my retracting blade,
and swung my iron bar to break its ribs,
but notice I have brought along my notepad,
to record the mayhem and observe
my own extremely small, in fact, barely detectable,
feeling of transgression.
What a precious thing that little feeling is,
look how it perches on my shoulder,
nodding and chirping while I smash the couch!

Orphée

The time I bought a full-length mirror,
it barely fit in the car.
I had to pull the booster chair,
uproot the headrests
and recline the seat to lay it flat
like a long unbending body
rectangled in black,
with its feet toward the back.

It was a good passenger,
no trouble at all.
At every stop light I would look
over my shoulder at it,
and each time it was just lying there,
stiff as a pharaoh,
looking up through the sunroof at nothing,
at whatever was above us in the sky
as we went by.

Prone, with the long clouds
dashing across it, a mirror
is a little like a girl
lying in the sun,
and also a little like
the swimming pool she is beside,
with that deepening calm just under
the restless surface,
where the searching and elastic light
relaxes into settled blue.
I think the girl is you.

Now it stands in the bedroom,
remembering those clouds,

and reflecting on the day
of its abduction, when it lay
for nearly an hour in the glare
under the great, harsh sun
and gathered every bit of it in
and gave every bit of it back.
Before the new life began,
in the dim room
with the curtains drawn,
and the man who comes to stare
at something he wants in there.

Shadowed

A cougar will attack from behind,
I'm told, and it will feel
like somebody cracking a two-by-four
over the back your neck.
Later, you may show the reporters twenty-nine
neat metal staples down your spine,
and what you will say is: I guess it just wasn't
my time.
And later still, in the deep night,
you will be alone with the uncontrollable
shaking, but that isn't you being afraid
of a lion, it is only your body,
that great confused baby,
attempting to figure things out,
too simple to know
that the past
has passed.

Anyway, it is something to think about
as I walk too quickly
up this gravel road, alone.
Except, it is regret
that is stalking me
with quiet steps,
while the past keeps pace
in the steep bluffs and dark foliage
on either side.

Middle Age

If you have ever tried
to climb a slide,
(along the slippery,
not the stepped
or staggered, side)
in your hard shoes, crawling
like a short-armed beetle
on the battered metal
(coming pretty close to falling!)
you will know just how it is
when you have reached the top
and stop
to look around,
from your place of high
accomplishment & pride,
at the low-down dirty ground
on every side,
and must now decide
what would be sadder,
to come down all at once
or take the ladder?

Life Science

Some question there was, you will recall,
about what kind of thing a man
might be, whether a
damaged angel or aspiring beast,
but it turns out we are all
deuterostomes, that is,
"beings whose mouths come second," meaning
that in our embryonic phase the anus
unfurls first, a trait we share with starfish
and the spiked echinoderms;
whereas, among the annelids and snails
and also the lobster with his horrid, restless face,
it is the mouth that comes before.
But we are all, in any case,
tube-things, organized with
hunger at one end and dispossession at the other,
and having life requires the constant
pushing of matter through these central pipes,
which we accomplish, in the way of our kind,
by moving waste from mouth to tail,
as do the sessile serpulids,
the big-eyed suction-footed squids
and eke the nightingale,
but not the sponge.

And here is where the systematic mind
must ask: are these good things
to know? That we are, in the transverse axis,
asymmetrical, as time itself is, too,
our mouth-parts deep
in the approaching day and long tails lashing
in the past, and what one calls
one's life is something like a duct
through which desire is made substantial,
then extruded in the form of loss —

well, these are notions
nobody will murder you for not believing,
for the sake of which no man
will torch another's roof,
or raise a pile of limestone to the sky,
but why, if any of it is true, would I
feign seriousness?
Is there some reason I don't spend my day
rolling my pottery tub around the block
and cackling and pointing
at the great plucked hen
that styles itself "a Man"?
For, if we are not just food for worms
as poets and smirking churchmen say,
but worms ourselves,
then what unfurls behind me on my way
through life, as I go slithering
forth through it,
can only be, forgive me, shit.

But now I will do something
which you may think is just
a yielding to weak sentiment,
or a salesman's trick,
slapping a coat of moral uplift
on this nihilist tirade,
but I am within my rights to do it,
indeed it is as much my nature
as the chameleon's is to gobble flies.

I will tell you that we have inside us
something that evades detection,
something lithe and featureless
and fearless which adores its life

not as a whale loves krill
or as a serpent loves
its own hilarious elongation,
but as one loves a helpless child,
pretending to be wise for its sake,
giving it not just sustenance
but guidance, teaching it
the way to be alive.

Fortune's Algorithm

If only you could strip
off the falseness,
tear away its fabulous
headgear and expose
the good bald head.
Pull off the cloak
of cockatiel feathers,
the pleated wimple
sewn by cunning devils
and detach its pride
and joy, the superbly long
and decorative but useless
tail. Pluck the fobs,
pull down the bunting,
plaster swags, mahogany
festoons and all. An end
to bewilderments,
now we shall take
the thing as it is,
boiled down to the strict
it of itself and see
the moist worm that is
down there slim
and gleaming, which is
all that was worth keeping
when the rest was tossed,
what we found
under the oiled
musculature, the reticulated
scales and dorsal fan, when we
peeled those away.
                    There
it was, fluttering shyly,

thin as air and faintly
bioluminescent like a naked
fairy, crouching in the cup
of a tulip... but without
the cocked cap folded
from a leaf, and no wings
either, or even a human
shape, oh the dazzlements
and distractions, finding
myself wherever I look,
as if each thing should have
hands and feet and be a sort
of small me, my selves
all around, diminutive
and large, but those go too,
as we burrow down to our
fusiform truth, purer
than Brancusi's polished steel
plantain or larval snail or
whatever it was supposed to be,
for even that has edges
and makes a shape
against its background,
and what we are after
is less than a faint dusting
of blue light in a dark
and quiet room, a pulsing
hum from a faraway machine.
Or something hard perhaps
but elemental, clean
and penetrating like a quill,
the song cut down to one note,
the poem reduced to its one
good word, the word
that says it all.

But what is beneath it
may not be words at all,
but a concisely coded
algorithm like the one
for generating Voronoi diagrams,
presented by Steven Fortune in
*Proceedings of the second
annual symposium
on Computational geometry,*
1986, which gives,
bear with me, rules
for enclosing a random
scattering of points
in lines, a patch of code
as perfect as a sonnet,
that sweeps your screen
like a magician's cape,
exposing the secret
intelligibility of the brown
cracked-tile design
on a giraffe's orange hide,
the tesselations on a turtle's back,
the polygons that just appear
in fields of drying mud
soap bubbles and the cell
walls of a pubescent leaf,
familiar patterns, governed by
an unfamiliar logic;
and the same math optimizes
wireless coverage and
makes sense of how
a small medieval town
acquires its shape, and plots
the proximity of victims
to a cholera-infected well ...

and I'm using a lot of words
to explain this, but what it seems to show
is that beneath the sprawl and jumble
of it all, there might be
something small and true,
a clean understandable perch
where the tired mind can rest
a moment as it wanders through
the shambling ruin of its world
and *that*, surely, is the cold
bonework of the real,
the very frame on which the braids
and draperies are hung,
a formula that can be read
and used and understood —

though admittedly nothing
stays understood for long, and even
this small thing grows
stems again and spreads
and sprouts, Delaunay
triangulations and techniques
for teaching robots how to move,
and the unmemorizable
names and hideous beards
of German mathematicians,
and every last thing sprouts antlers,
it all grows forks and tines
and casts itself into the widening
frazzle, so a thing and the best
way to describe it
are one proliferating snarl
that fans like Barnsley's ferns,

or flies apart like the exploding
pods of the obscenely vital
jewel weed whose fleshy children
rise together in a fetid tangle
in the low spots at the edges
of my garden, sliding roots
deep in the misleading
simplicity of the
good black earth.

Entities

"Sometimes it is desired that a person can establish a long-term relationship (such as a reputation) with some other entity, without necessarily disclosing personally identifying information to that entity. In this case, it may be useful for the person to establish a unique identifier, called a pseudonym, with the other entity."
— WIKIPEDIA

Enough is enough. When I joined this group
I had one small question about grafting tomatoes.
"Need Help Preventing Corky Root"
was how I put it, and thanks for the prompt answer,
Bloody Butcher, you are not the problem here,
I took your advice on perlite and it worked,
and at that point, as Banana Legs has said
I should have retreated to my potting shed,
but then I came across that very long exchange
where Beefsteak lectured Ponderosa Pink
on downy mildew and the southern blight,
which turned somehow into a fight
about the Civil War, and I have family in the South,
the most unracist people you could hope to meet,
so I just had to have my say, and Autumn Sugar,
bless her, backed me all the way,
about which time it just came out
that Dwarf Champion repudiates the Lord, which is his right
but is rude about it, which you don't have to be
and it seems clear now that he would rather fight
than just agree — as I have said ten times! — to disagree.
Well, I don't have to remind this bunch that words
are all we share, a few good words between us,
and the bad ones just demean us,
and what more could you ask for? Well,
since you had to bring that up, I feel I need
the soil between my fingers, ell-oh-ell,
black earth and worms and the reason we are here:

tomatoes. Tomatoes, people!
Therefore, consider this goodbye.
No backward looks. I'm particularly glad
to have met some of you, I'm thinking here of
Mister Stripey, Matchless Taste and Love-Me-Do.
Tigerella, you can fuck yourself. As for the rest of you,
as the song says, I may be hard,
but that don't mean I'm hard to please.
Whatever that may mean. So long, Pard.
If anybody wants me I'll be on my knees
in my back yard.

Gardening in Late Winter

The snow is moulting, and the air smells weird.
Winter is dribbling back into the sewers,
and last year's leaves have lately reappeared,
to ripen brownly, as the month matures.
It's actually hot! My neighbour's in his shirt,
shifting snow so he can touch the dirt,
and beads of sweat are dripping from his beard.
The sun's revolving on its sharpened pole,
looking as if it plans to eat us whole.
I know my garden's down there, brown and wet
and waiting where I left it. Yet,
a little snow still hides my turnip beds.
The hill is still a little white, the kids
are running to it with their wooden sleds.
Run, children! Ride 'em if you've got 'em!
It's all downhill from Paradise to Sodom.
Let's plant those jingling stockings on our heads
and ride our long toboggans to the bottom!

My Real Estate Agent's Kitchen

> ... *the earth*
> *And common face of Nature spake to me*
> *Rememberable things; sometimes, 'tis true,*
> *By chance collisions and quaint accidents ...*
> — WILLIAM WORDSWORTH, *THE PRELUDE*

So this is about a small joke the world played on me.
It's a story I've had with me for a while.
I've tried it out, now and again,
and moved it back and forth,
the way you carry a sick plant from room to room
following sunlight around the house
but I am tired of hints and riddles,
I am tired of effortful elaboration
and the effort of concealment, too.
I will tell it plainly, this time. It begins
in a stand of pines
where I'd gone once or twice, as a teen.
There was a creek running through it.
I drank from the questionable
brown stream to prove to myself I belonged there
and ate raw fiddleheads to show
the plants did not hate me,
but they were bracken ferns, as I now know,
and supposedly toxic, and the stream
was a cattle wallow, yet it did me no harm.
I sat down in a cave of roots
and gave names to the landscape around me,
and was enjoyably alone all afternoon,
claiming the place as my own.

And for some reason it became a dream I go back to,
a place with layers, a deep turf
in the thatch of my sleep,
where the ritual of recognition is performed,
over and over.

And finding myself there, or finding "there"
in myself, if you prefer,
night after night,
comes with an odd weightless sensation,
as if the word "again" could stand alone,
againness hanging in the air.
Here, again. This, again. Again.
Although sometimes in the dream
I am trying to get there,
crossing a self-editing field of the mind, overgrown
with buckthorn and scrub willows,
and nothing is where it belongs,
the cicadas are silent, the path is a blur,
and the moment — so familiar — when it all suddenly seems
so familiar, won't come.

Then, thirty years later, my nights
perturbed mainly by restless children,
and needing a nice town for them
to be periodically asleep in,
we came back to live not too far from those pines,
just a short drive from the dream place, in fact,
but by then what remained of the woods
had a highway on top of it,
and the creek now flowed through a galvanized culvert
with a grate at each end,
and while we were looking around
for a good house to live in
our real estate agent drove us right down the road
and right through the "rememberable" place,
and there we all were in the wakeful present,
moving at tremendous speeds,
a flush of Fords and Corollas
and Daewoos and Chryslers
streaming through the scarves and tatters
of my sleep.
   And we had no luck at all
finding a house, so on the way back

we stopped at hers for some coffee, and here
I come to the part of the story
that is pure nonsense. She gave us
the tour of her house, with its posts and its beams,
and the half bath, and the full bath,
and the honey-gold country-style cabinets
her husband had made from some wood
that was milled, we were told, from a stand
of old pines that had had to come down
when the highway went in,

                       and so,

in addition to having a road
through it, my strange and private
dream was now
rails and stiles and floating panels
and a convenient kidney-shaped counter
in my real estate agent's kitchen.

Ghosts

"You're lucky to believe in ghosts,"
she told my girl.
"Losing fear, as I did, has a cost.
When you are older, you may find you've lost
wonderment along with terror,
faith with foolishness and error.
One goes as the other goes.
Even the crows, this spring, sound just like men
pretending to be crows."

Really There

To bite an apricot, or sail
a complicated little boat,
or tune a drumskin, is to fail
to have a use for words
like love, fortuity,
forgiveness, or the future.
It is to not need something
said another way,
or to be stirred
to capture some elusive
feature of it, to evade cliché,
or, falling short, to have to say
"the thought falls short"
or "words cannot convey,"
and let the facts collapse
upon themselves
yet not regret some
lapse of aptness
in the scattered wreck,
or feel the damp hand
of an unarticulated something
settle on your neck.

But now, suppose you stroll
across a dam at night,
a humid summer night,
a little wind in your sleeves,
and stop to lean across the rail
to look down at the stream,
pulled placid and black
up to the worn concrete lip,
and you can just make out
the rafts of foam
and the sliding skin
being sucked calmly
over the edge in the dark

and hear from somewhere below
the roar as it shatters
itself and is pulled apart,
the black river rumbling
in the shins of your legs.

It turns out you do
need words for that,
or somehow none of it is
really there.

Ephemeroptera

"*Things are more like they are now
than they ever were before.*"
— DWIGHT D. EISENHOWER

The girl who came and found the castle empty,
found supper on a sideboard and the clocks
all stopped; a ring of keys, the candles lit
a change of clothing and a place to sit
beneath a lancet window overlooking
forking paths and brambly paths
and cultivated plots (and far away
some little man-shaped figures stooking hay
and others tending geese,
or kneeling at a brook
or lifting limestone on a cantilevered hook)
and she leaned out to feel the sun,
searching the valley with a *searching* look
and asked herself: Am I inside a book?
It seemed to be the case
that things she hadn't planned had taken place.
And this appeared to be the place they took.
And she would seem to be the one
to whom the things that happen
happen. So …

the girl put on the clothes and ate the food
and wound the clocks, and went from room to room
trying her chain of keys in all the locks.
And she found nothing anywhere
but treasure-chests and mirrors, treasure,
chairs, more treasure, mirrors, and a chair —
no secret door, no crystal stair,
no silver ladder spun from human hair,
and no way out.

For the story is a gracious captor,
but there are things it can't permit.
It must insist on being what it is
and stifle anything that isn't it.
There will be paths you shouldn't follow
games you cannot win,
thoughts you'd be advised to never have,
and rooms you'd really better not go in
lest you should hasten
the arrival of the moment when
it tells you in that slow, clear voice,
that solemn, storytelling voice,
"I'm afraid that you have left me little choice ..."

Whereas the world outside those walls
has neither plot nor thought,
and leaves no pattern but its own
proliferating weirdness, leaving room
for all the unwholesome forms a fact might take —
the pygmy hog, the milk-eyed snake
catfrog and kettlebird, oryx and crake,
the socknecked half-immortal turtle,
bagfaced batfish, the felicitously fertile
German roach, and the little temporary ones
the fairy-winged ephemeroptera,
those beautiful losers, mayflies that may fly
ninety minutes till they mate and die
and fall back in their sedimented lake
(where even yet these evanescent
beings may persist
as little forktailed fossils,
rockbound in the schist).
And in the middle distance, in the mist
where the wide horizon turns to haze,
other lives are going other ways
and other worlds are yearning to exist.

There, in the cool dominions of the muse,
master artificers are making news.
Ambitious young musicians scour the score
in search of music never heard before —
caprices in the key of L,
duets for Windsor chair and kitchen floor,
pegleg partitas and Volkswagen blues,
and everyone is busy forcing more
and stronger, stranger stuff
into a world that was already full enough.

And now the girl (as I was saying)
came to the highest tower
and found herself before
a slotted window in a sunlit hall
under the lintel of the last unopened door.
And there she hesitated as a tall
stalk of sunlight moved across the wall
slipping sideways, brick by brick
like a finger following a hidden text,
sliding toward the thing that happened next.
She put the key in, and she heard it click.

("A poem, containing the titles of five Canadian novels.")

I Will Meet You There

You can come by road but it is better
to go by way of the boxwood maze,
counting your steps, making your
choices and being either right or wrong.
Start from a wild guess, proceed
to the obvious, turn sooner than you meant to,
backtrack, pause,
zoom forward, retreat, start fresh.

Or come to me over the field, singing in Gaelic,
swishing the tall grass this way and that.
When you arrive at the fence,
cut a hole in the fence
and drive your reindeer through but do not follow.
Soon you may come to a place you know,
cross over it boldly, and with each step
say goodbye, and no more,
goodbye, goodbye.

It will not be there when you turn around.
And when you come to a river,
ford the stream where it casts
its little chattering faces over the rocks,
feel your way through the reeds at the far side,
you will find a small boat
and there is a word on the transom,
read it or not, as you wish, you will not
remember it. Now, follow the stream's
toothy dazzle, and do not
lose your way in the current, be diverted
but never beguiled,

keep track of the broken-up light here
where the black stream
crumples like a sheet of zinc
and shift your bare feet in the schooling shadows,

memorize ways as you go,
count the wrong turns, correct any errors,
run if you can, rest if you must.
You may find pumpkins swelling provocatively
on the banks, enjoy them freely, freely dally
among the pumpkins for a while, then
take your leave and you will not be asked
to talk about it later. Carry on. The limbs of the trees
hang low, the alders are thick. The rocks are sharp
and the mosses are up to your hips.

Smile. Growl. Go down on all fours,
go down with the sow bugs, the old
gill-breathing fourteenipede creatures unchanged
since the babbling infancy of the world, when life
was a schoolchild's caprice, and stand there till your eyes ache
from peering into the darkness
and your chest hurts from holding in the truth
and the grief sinks deeper in you than your bones
and all we have lost
wells up where your heart was,
and that is where I will be, waiting.

Life Throes:
Selected Poems

Camels nor Millionaires

"... plants and animals will altogether cease after the renewal of the world."
— ST. THOMAS AQUINAS

No tyger tygers in our hereafter,
nor wee sleekit beasties, nor darkling thrush.
No Leviathan, no Conqueror Worm.
No Three Bears.

No Moroccan spider that rolls like a wheel;
no bird that weaves leaves;
no creature that does not actually fly,
that is wrongly considered venomous,
regurgitates when threatened
or is boneless, segmented
and eats dung.

Arriving, expect not to find
lions, long-legged beasts
nor anything to ask deliverance from.
Nor shall the holy be mediated through
unwholesome extremes or pointless monstrosities,
prehensile tails and proboscides,
serrated tongues, tentacles, egg-sacs,
multiple stomachs, specialized prongs
for rooting up ferns. All these

we leave at the turnstile
with our gold teeth and trophies.
Let them pass. Experts and curiosity seekers
do not prosper in Heaven.
Your thoughts run to nothing specific.
The talk is confined
to that one one-syllable word
pronounced in an eerie vibrato.
You will not have facts
or fingertips
or keep a little dog
hidden from the concierge.

To My Body

I address you directly, Jack
my dumb pony; for once
answer me back.
I fill you with helium, dunce,
and hang you up slack,
perpendicular to heaven,
an intimate sack
of urges —
        who needs who?
I sing God's praises. You are my kazoo.

My implement, I stand you up
thrumming with inane vigour
beneath me, noisily inert,
like a tossed pitchfork
quivering in the dirt.
I choose where to put you. I, Bopeep
receive your broadcast,
push your button. Beep.
When you hurt
(you should hear yourself howl)
I crank prayers like pasta through the mouth of you;
I weep you when you weep;
I repent of you always, but
remove you only when I sleep.

With your
vocabulary of spasms,
your yammering heart,
the gnash of signals, the grope,
the resolute grope of sensation,
is it me you address,
O my envelope?
Each day you are less.
Do you know that you're falling apart?
The life you transmit,

the *life* you transmit
was a blank to me right from the start.
I understand nothing of it.

Speak up, my pod my pod;
I never paid to ride on you.
You pitch us headlong at the sod
hut cannot holler loud enough for two.
Always I catch you fingering the knots.
Our ends connect. Do you see?
They connect.
Pause, please. Ruminate. Reflect.
Roll your eyes back in their slots,
can you detect
me, gaseous me, thinking your thoughts?

Shed

Spacecraft require maintenance, as do
nuclear submarines. A shed is not
a pressurized enclosure and neglect
makes it beautiful.

Jet cars, hydrofoils, get there. A shed stays
put or conveys
what's in it between days at the safe
velocity of its decay.

Carbon steel, vanadium steel,
are impervious. A shed's made of
wood, glass
patched with newsprint,
an early, not very reliable
kind of scotch tape,
square-headed nails, boot rivets and tin,
any of which can withstand only
a very small range
of temperatures and conditions.

Skewed doorframes, warped boards,
a hole for the stovepipe,
leak light
and little tag ends of sky
come in under the sills,
tingeing the shelved preserves.

Sidereal clocks, atomic chronometers
record intervals, and forget them
immediately. A shed
rots at no fixed rate,
and each alteration can be read
in its collapse, in its becoming
feature by feature
gradually not a shed.

Les Souvenirs

Here a shop has, and sells for twelve ninety five,
handcrafted in Canada,
free-standing baby-faced Indian dolls.
They balance on slices of birch,
clasping suede-tipped arrows,
bows strung up with yarn
and little handbags on a string.
They have headbands, stamped
with a pattern of canoes
and coats of mauve leather
scored with glitter and fringed.
They are all female and all
very young; real beads
hang from their pigtails, glued
to their outsized brown plastic heads,
cheeks puffed out in a fixed kiss,
wide eyes engineered to roll in their whites
when you shake them. Shake them
and they look alive;
lie them down and their eyelids
close and they won't
disappoint you.

Social Studies

"This is your history," said the teacher of it.
And it was. So, now, is she,
passing around her portrait of a Cree
Indian in a top hat. Any child could see
how meticulously bad that drawing was:
a face like a heraldic shield,
with stuck-on eyes and cheeks of pencil fuzz;
a mouth of line, and, dangling beneath,
a canted Celtic alphabet of teeth.
In hands like dinner forks it seemed to hold
a strip of parchment, sumptuously scrolled;
and this, Miss Ward revealed to us, revealed,
in Bible Gothic, signed with an x and sealed,
how Indians had given up the deeds
to our dominion, in return for beads.

Beside the blackboard, maps were tacked
which showed the world cut up like orange rind,
sliced and sectioned, air-brushed, dotted lined
and crammed with calculations to distract
each young, impressionable mind
from the corrupt, the riotously inexact
contours of unornamented fact.
For there on the grid, like a spilled drink:
the land of Canada, vast and milkshake pink,
pocked with lakes spattered with islands that had lakes,
a pattern of mistakes within mistakes,
profusely annotated with the names of towns,
Manigotagan, Flin Flon, Churchill Downs,
stuck like mayflies in a web of red
roads and rails, unravelling like thread
among the moraines and glacier melts,
dust bowls, tree lines, lichen belts,
along the flumes and gravel beds

where European traders packed their pelts
across our atlas, laying traps
to capture beavers when there were no maps.

Our history, I'll be honest, is at most
a theory which the facts do not confute.
Some people came from somewhere to a coast
as ragged as the salt line on a boot,
and pitched their cabins in the wilderness,
and did the things that somehow led to this.

The country I live in is a patch of thorns
below a culvert in a sunken plot
where burly geese with necks like flugelhorns
intimidate the pigeons and are shot
by a district sales manager named Russ.
And that's it. Our lives, our landscape, us.
But near the train yard, where I catch my bus,
a late October frost has clenched the ground,
the football field is hard as frozen meat,
enormous gulls are swaggering around
with snowflakes on their orange rubber feet.
They cruise through stubble with their beaks ajar
shrieking that what they are they are they are.

400 Jobs in Murdochville

From the post-card town of Gaspé
a filament of road unspools toward
Murdochville, dangled in deepest scrub
like a hooked fish that nobody is bothering
to reel in. And the city just hangs,
while the mine closes
and the jobs go poof
and the houses literally leave town,
plucked from their foundations
and packed off on flatbeds
to the coast.

Murdochville sits in a natural ashtray
between hills, on a mountain of soot.
The mine-shafts slither down
from the number one crater,
around which the orange toy dumptrucks spiral
on ramps of smoking crud.
The pit radiates death
to the surrounding landscape, creating
a vast suburb of killed spruce around Murdochville,
standing barkless and bone-dead
and full-grown, as if they'd grown up dead
from dead seeds and spread dead over
the charred marshmallow of the hills —
"It used

to be worse," the school principal tells me,
"You couldn't even grow a lawn." But now,
thankfully, the mines are closing and small trees
flourish again in the empty lots;
and each night the town
gives off less light, as somebody else's front window
winks out for good.
Nobody was born here,

but some are determined to stay.
They go on
putting in lawns, and waiting for news,
their satellite dishes
all turned the same way,
cupping their ears to the outside world.

Foreigners

Their architecture intrigues us;
their regional specialties too
are an education;
amazed that they eat bugs,
still, we appreciate the wisdom
of adapting to difficult circumstances,
of burrowing homes into the rock,
gathering cow dung for fuel,
and being the first to invent the astrolabe;
of subsisting on cabbage-wine and strong cheeses,
worshipping in the cult of a Local Variant,
evolving a form of money too heavy to lift.

That they stare back at us
is very pleasing.
We are delighted to be delightful;
in their presence
we savour our own
oddness, an engaging sensation;
especially, we love to excuse
their attitudes and beliefs,
indigenous quirks
in the costume of
Immanent Values or Eternal Verities,
like the man in the mud mask
who says he's a god.
Who are we to argue?

It is worth losing a snapshot
to be told by the subject
he is afraid for his soul.

A Word I Dislike

Honesty! It sounds like a last gasp
A truncated sermon. A yawn
cut short by oof the mortal thrust.
That ghost of an aitch;
that donkey-bray nasal;
those gossipy esses and tees:
even the noise of it
begs your divulgence —
even the sound says please.

A word with strange cravings,
one that
solemnly lifts up skirts
with the tip of an umbrella,
that fumbles at clasps, and
uncorks over cocktails;
a word that yearns

a) to be whisked off its feet
b) to be thumbed through
c) to be psychoanalyzed

Try looking glad when you say it.

Now sneaky
is a word that smiles for the camera.
Sneaky's intact:
its nose has never been busted;
its Pepsodent pearlies
run like a picket, clear round
to the back of its head.
It looks both ways,
knows all the ins and the outs,
and finds itself more near and dear
than bumpkin honesty
to that bold Viking, Truth.

Reminiscence of My Childhood
Viking Winter

The men sit around in their pronged hats
getting on with the era.
Nothing much is accomplished.
They eat dried fish and feed the heads
to the king's imported dog;
they squat in corners of the great hall, squinting
in the wintry light that comes in
under the skewed beams, and through chinks
in the sill, whittling house-gods from old
tether posts and broken oars;

they wolf down skimpy suppers and lean
over the big table, talking seriously about
becoming Christians.

Sometimes they fret with ropes
or scrape down their salt-stiffened breeches
pretending to wish
they were at sea.

At night they hold contests
of lifting anvils
and catching hot coals,
and contest of poetry, telling
what squalls they have weathered,
what deaths averted, and what a lasting death
we anyway come to.

The wives turn spits and spin wool —
they are sometimes mentioned in the stories,
turning, they are sometimes mentioned,
but they ignore the stories.
Even the queen ignores the stories.

When it is late
we lie together on the cloth mats
hugging each other for warmth
till sleep, our sanctioned
delirium, creeps up in her black smock
and gently separates us like strips of felt
suspending each
in his private darkness.

Our oblivions have no edges
yet they do not merge.
I cannot say what dreams we have.
I know only my own.

Reminiscence of My Childhood
Changes of Weather

Rainclouds pending.

The Inca pavilion sweats in its lichen
and crack
    ! lightning strikes the big lintel,
monsoon drops like molly's bloomers
from a bank of fog.

The jungle mossily exults

and all plant life, languid and nerveless,
rears up with muscles of wind:
twigs fly out of the thatch,
flower petals rise like a swarm of bees,
the meek trees fling off their monkeys,
emitting a powerful noise.

A sound like laughter from
old sedentary logs
unlodged from the mud
and rising in the rising swamp.

Sedge grass flails at the brink of the flood.
A bracelet of frog's eggs
snagged to a sunken frond
revolves almost peacefully
                in the brown water.

Tzigli-Qelotl
holds her hands over her ears
as her hut pops its wattles
and the rain washes corn from her bowl.

Outside,
    the men dance,
bouncing like hailstones in the clearing.
They are daubed with blood, they
become powerful as the storm itself
because they are at its mercy.

Reminiscence of My Childhood
Old Love Song

O sullen one, put on your mask
and the feathered shoulder-ornament,
the elegant shoulder-ornament,
then dance for my corn-privilege
                in the gathering place.

Why do you not come?
                Brother, why do you not
eat momal and trample the young roots?
I waited for you
in the dust at the path's edge
when the pounding-work was finished.

The evening came
                driving her red cow.
The moon came,
                she was not too busy,
but Brother you did not come.

Reminiscence of My Childhood
Dionysian Revels

Horse legs and face of a regular guy,
in runs the somebody whatsmith from next door
and tells me the Titans are rioting in the hills
and they'll rip off our cocks
if we don't get packing,
and I'm damned if I want to go
but I'm wondering what to do with
my original Phidias of myself
when the matter's decided:
there's a noise like dice
from outside, a clatter in the tiled hall,
here they come, I think, sticking
my head out, the whole town
must be in it together,
and no gods but
thirty significant dolts
joined at the loins, swarm forward,
knocking the plates off my walls.
They seize my little Ion,
and carry him off. I haven't seen him since.
And from there it got worse.

None of that makes me forget
how it once was.
There was an air to it, and not
just trouble: one drop
and we'd been of the very goat,
such was our faith.
We brought our own table to the High Town
and were up till the sun eating lambs,
and in the morning the poor of the city
crept in to suck on our napkin stains.

Reminiscence of My Childhood
Things that Persist

When I was a child in Baghdad
a brass winch drew the barges
up the speckled Euphrates
(or was it the Tigris?), slow as a sundial
as I watched from the colander spire
under the painted-on zodiac
in the company of my father's advisors;
and my five private identical tutors
looked on through electrum telescopes, sighing:

Lania, Hagoi, lania, lania, hara' cthoth-oi

The tower was high and the door to my chamber
was barred and guarded and four deaf-mutes
stood by while I bathed or read books
or composed rishum.
I was never permitted to leave.
More than once I leaned on the worn stone rail
over the garden, steeling my nerve,
gazing down on soldiers
and diplomats circulating
in hats shaped like gelatin molds
among fountains and pheasants
and basalt tubs, tufted with palms,
straining to hear, hearing:

Lania, Hagoi, lania, lania, hara' cthoth-oi

The sailors called out in Italian
(or was that French?) to our citizens' wives
and were slaughtered at dawn
by decree of the Lesser Caliph,
with his Book of Commands
and his potions of eternal youth
and his writhing retinue of gauzy concubines
asleep with their eyes open on red cushions,

singing:

Lania, Hagoi, lania, lania, hara' cthoth-oi

But those days are gone.
Three times we've been conquered since then.
The Khan wrecked our canals,
the topsoil blew west
and most of us left there for here.
I will never be accustomed to snow.
The bank closed my grocery store.
My hands shake,
I forget things.

Loss, o Beloved, loss, loss,
look what has been taken from us.

Reminiscence of My Childhood
Petit Marcel

Drawn and perpetually re-drawn
in that faintly-remembered beige pastel
on the paper with the art-museum shield stamped on it,
a portrait of a forgotten lady
from the court of a Louis greater I think than twelve
but less than fourteen, and the crippled conçierge
come in at nine, to draw the crêpes
against the sun and shut the clangers
one by one, raising a hood of grey powder.
At noon: the rigid *au pair* on her knees
eye level with the undersag of the chaise longue,
getting the heaves out of the rug
on the unravelled patch where the two-clawed console
(under the clock shaped like Chartres)
gathers the tough grey fibres.

At three I'm alone to float
through the mirrored doors. My reflection
swarms up at my back, with menacing gesticulations.
I sail like a bubble
from one room to the next
on the locked top floor,
isolating in my perfect eyesight
the pale map of China
crazed like bone china,
the bottomless umbrella jug,
the window that undulates the back garden
overlooking the walk.
What a view! a potting shed,
a rotten hole in the rattan throne,
cavities of rust in the white cast iron bench.
Decaying pears.

In the evening it is cool enough to go outside
and sit by the pond.
You can tell where the carp are
by the lilies.
I have certain chores.
Today I raked leaves.
Tomorrow I dress the fire for All-Souls.
There are logs that for no reason at all
won't burn.

Tackle

Lifting a grisly clump
of snarled lures from the box,
I am startled at the mock
vigour of their life
throes. The bulb-eyed
hyena-coloured
mannikin fish
attacks everything.
Stiff as a finger splint,
jointed with steel pins,
it grapples lead wire,
frogspawn and red spoons
in the sorting tray.
The spotted wriggler
cuddles a rubber
horsefly. Red
devils and beaded
spinners, abstract
as microbes,
invade one another.

There is also a white
spider
with a single barb
tucked under its thorax.
I select this one,
and lower it down nylon
into the lake.
Folding my hands on my chest
in the boat bottom,
I scrutinize clouds.

In the dark
under my back the spider
revolves on its glassy fibre,
succulent, murderous, attached.

Lovely

The past is lovely, it lasts forever.
Somewhere, I'm still
lying under the lawn sprinkler
with no Coppertone on,
the grass cool and elastic under my back,
a black spaniel nuzzling my feet.
The cars are old-fashioned and optimistic,
the people who drive them
have fallen in love with the future,
They can't know that when they get here
they will love the past more,
that the present will look like
a stupendous machine
for forcing things to stop existing.
Well, to live for the moment
is best, but the moments, the little
jiffies, they are startled
to be here, like
the high-shouldered cuprous beetles
that live beneath patio stones,
if you're curious you lift one up
and let it run down your arm.
The other ones scoot for cover,
struggling down into the leaf mulch,
kicking frantically.

The Slough

Are the entrails clear, immaculate cabbage?
— THEODORE ROETHKE, "UNFOLD! UNFOLD!"

What's under the pudding skin, down in the slough
where the weed-pods root whose heads poke through
to goggle and bob in their seedy hats,
pithless and punch-drunk, chewed by gnats,
knocked flat by a damp, disagreeable breeze,
gusts of bad weather, abrupt as a sneeze
and stilt-birds sunk to their bamboo knees
in whatever is under the slough?

What's under the mud that schmecks our boots?
A raft of bedsprings lashed with roots,
spavined lumber, cans of glue,
electrical cables, lampreys, newts,
and, if what the neighbours say is true,
the ribs of a horse that once fell through
while pursuing a dog, who's in there too:
so all poor beasts that flit or thud
lie down with the frogs in the lathered mud,
who mate in the ruts where the tractor treads,
spin their milky, gelatinous threads
of spunk and spittle and clean, green eggs
that hatch like bean-sprouts, sprout hind legs
and rise, scientifically, out of the ooze
to walk upright in soft-soled shoes
and ponder the matter of what or who's
in the slough.

Off in the aftermath, what's up there?
A million metric tons of air.
Peacocks in the weeping figs
amble through a land of twigs
and flocks of phosphorescent, screaming
crook-nosed parrots copulate

upside down inside the gleaming
spirals of an iron gate.
Plying the trackless, gassy skies,
the wild cranes have crazy eyes
and jagged claws and skinny necks.
The natural world is quite complex.
Praising nature, one suspects
the Lombardy poplars pitch and sway
because these trees are having sex
with other trees three miles away.
Help me Ted, my days are dense
with moments that do not make sense!
Where is the love that spins the gears,
that honks the goose and flaps the crane
and cranks the sun and other stars
across the crinkled diaphane?
Where is the foot that pumps the treadle?
Whose the hand that tracks the moth?
Who scales the wooden frame of evening
tacking bolts of yellow cloth?
Who ignores this? When is ever?
Why am I stupid? What is true?
None of that transmutes to answers
anywhere next to, beneath, or on top of,
over or under the slough.

March 1

Sometime today I'm turning 35.
The cover of Time would like to know
"When Did the Universe Begin?"
God would tell us if he were alive.

If God were alive I'd tell him where to go.
I guess I'd go to Maui if I could,
get away from all this fucking snow.
I think Hawaiians make their gods from wood,

a friend of mine has got one on a shelf.
I'd find it strange to get down on my knees
in front of something that I'd carved myself.
Skip a step, perhaps, and worship trees.

The universe has been in style this year,
you run across it in the magazines.
No one wonders why the thing is here
or whether it will end in smithereens,

but when, exactly, did it first appear?
I gather it's unfolding. Earlier today,
my mother called me on the phone to say
I'd used up half of my "allotted span."

How long since whoever made it first began
decanting eons from the crystal flask?
You wouldn't think a magazine called "Time"
would have to ask.

Spring

The first banjo chords of spring after that endless
fugue on the hydraulic organ.
Dogs are running with their leashes off.
A skinny man
has dismantled his motorcycle in the sun.
A child is not wearing mitts.
It's my child
with a plastic shovel,
pushing some carbonized snow
over the curb.

Someone I know well is down in his basement
going through boxes.
He is sitting in a big pile of letters,
yearbooks, notepads,
figure drawings in orange conté,
things he has kept in case.

Nobody can say how he ended up here
with these boxes
and the whir of the gas furnace,
the faint, faraway sound
of children shrieking.

It is this sound
that he is listening to, and
I recognize the look
on his face, I've seen it before —
a focused grief, no
puzzlement, no
I've seen it before, oh yes
on a child trying to reattach
a doll's arm.

Tomato Hornworm

At what age did I learn that life
was something you could fail at?
That a life conducted badly leads
to rooms with blankets on the windows,
suppers of hard-boiled eggs,
a townhouse hunched between the legs
of an electric pylon. Bingo dabbers.
Pants that won't stay up.
Years spent poking at a screen,
dislodging molecules of fun.

When I hear hailstones rattle on a skylight,
watch a red bug climbing up a stem,
or admire a Nile-shaped crack in my wall,
in what sense am I living well?

How many times must I have liked the wine
before I can honestly say
What years those were,
if only I had them back?

If three times in five the wine is astringent,
the blubber discoloured,
the eggs a bit off,
then in some sense I must have done this
wrongly, ruined a good life
with crummy selections, botched
my self-portrait
with unstable paints and a varnish
that everyone knew would turn black.

Now something is slowly moving across its life,
a tomato hornworm.
It seems to care which way it goes,
it wants to live well,
it appears not to know
how horrid it is no matter what it does.

Palais de Justice

They are here to be dealt with
on a weekday morning,
when the unemployed are still
climbing into their housecoats, and the employed
are opening their mail.
In the malls the steel grills are unrolling,
the new weather is on its way,
but here, instead of climbing on fire escapes
and pissing in phone booths,
the criminals wait for hours on plastic chairs
in a well-lit hall.
They have messy hair and tattoos,
and ought to be locked up,
but how obedient they are,
waiting their turn,
clutching the papers they were told to bring.
One is walking up and down,
tapping his thigh with a brochure,
his sneakers chirping on the marble floor.
Another is pulling hairs
from the back of his hand.

Something amazing is happening behind those doors.
Innocence is throttling guilt,
the jury is clacking its mouth-parts,
experts have wrapped a helpless man with silk.

But out here, the staff
are having a day on the job.
The law passes back and forth over our heads
like a xerox light, and everyone is led
to other rooms where they will stand in line
to sign whatever they are told to sign.

Idleness

Drawing a treble clef
on the wall with my eye,

squinting at a chandelier
till each bulb in its red fez sprouts
vibrating bristles,

counting flies in a museum cafeteria
next to a table
where two lovers are coming apart
with a long talk and whole minutes
of horrified silence:
they are doing this terrible thing,
unwrapping their sadness
and showing it
to one another.
It is so awful how their voices
tremble,
but notice
the idleness of their hands
stacking coins,
pushing crumbs with a bank card,
breaking chunks from the rim
of a disposable cup
and placing these inside the cup until
there isn't a cup to contain them,
just a small pile of styrofoam chips.

My Son

How much death in this small fist?
How much in twelve weeks of the summer,

in the black star-map of his footprint
pinned to the wall above my desk?

Fourteen pounds: I have a bag of rice
heavier than that.

Yesterday he fell, or I dropped him
three steps down to a slab of concrete.

I examined him well, he was still closed
and perfect all over,
not open at all. Nothing was different
but still I saw it,
how much death there was,
how all of it poured out, a cloud of moths
hiding the light.

Spook

There are things so close to you
they are amazing — something alien
in the back of your hand,
a wildness in your child's eyes.

Once I received a package in the mail
containing my own shoes.

Then, travelling on a bus at night
I spent a long time looking
at water drops branching on the window,
my huge spook moving
over miles of dark,
its eyes inscrutable.

Erythronium

I can never remember what the word "crepuscular" means, although I've looked it up a hundred times. I have heard about a man worse off than that. He was unable to have new memories at all. He could not learn a name or a face. A minute would pass and the friend was a stranger again, the old joke became funny. He kept finding out that his dear wife had died. Again and again, a grief that would never be old.

I would love to memorize the names of the fish and the birds. Last summer I learned the herbaceous perennials that grow in my town, and for a while I had them by heart. Then winter came and the foliage went under snow. By spring, some things I knew well had gone off into the strangeness, seeping away into my quiet house while I napped. A few days ago, I found myself mute before a flower I knew, a yellow one shaped like a pagoda.

The word "crepuscular" means "living in twilight." I find myself drifting along in this twilight, a small wind drying my eyes. I am holding a feather, which I must have found on the street back there. The neighbourhood is full of locked cars and half-naked children playing under streetlights. Two of the children are mine. Hosewater patters softly on the bricks. Shapes I don't recognize are coming toward me out of the twilight, waving as if they know me well.

Vocal Accompaniment

Thou need'st not ask of me
What this strong music in the soul may be!
— SAMUEL TAYLOR COLERIDGE

A melody is stuck in my head, a bad one,
some kind of deranged
circus tune played on a
steam-powered Symphonotron,
and it is making a mockery of my dejection.
The poets, the old ones, grievers of yore,
had better music
for their dolor, lacrimations
for the *viola d'amore,*
koto solos, billowing chorales,
whereas I feel awful to the tune of
mouth harps, glass flutes and
Hawaiian guitars.
It is not a dark night but a frenzied
hootenanny of the soul.
On the rolling boards
balloonoid sailors and their spindly gals
clobber stubble-chinned buffoons
with rubbery mallets.
"Reality's dark dream," as Coleridge called it
in the calcine deeps of his despair
seems horribly bright now,
big on the skins of the eye,
while the mind's ears are flapping in time to
asthmatic concertinas
and the shrill peening of steel drums.

Orangutans

We have come here for the peanuts and to meet
the mortified stares of the wild men,
quarantined on their island of packed dirt,
in their crater of painted cement
under the theatrical fork
of a plaster tree.

We have entrusted them with three tires,
a bundle of rope
and as much straw as they can use,

and with a little encouragement
they have manufactured
minute quantities of fun,
twirling a stem of clover,
patting a small pile of dust,
pouring sand over a beetle.

We have also built bleachers for ourselves
to make sure we are comfortable while we wait
for the interesting thoughts
we are planning to have
as we watch what the orangutans
do.

TV

Sometimes it seems to believe I am somebody else,
someone who wants to see strangers
wipe out in huge waves,
golden-haired dogs catching frisbees,
cars being lifted with gigantic magnets.

Sometimes it almost seems to know me, it shows
a hillside in China,
the pope in his street clothes,
the eyes of a rapist.

It is trying to be funny and all it wants in return
is some of my time,
which is fine, I don't think
I would have spent the day reading Aquinas
or putting up drywall.

Look, a lot of good teeth.
An interesting bulge.

There's quite a lot there if you know where to look.
A man with his jacket on fire,
a palm tree bending over, a heart
pumping in the surgeon's hand.

I have a feeling I've been here before.
None of it seems new.
But I seem to be dying just as quickly
no matter what I do.

Aha, the dog can open a cage with his mouth.
That woman is setting them straight.
Cars are flying overhead in slow motion.

The same things happen here
as anywhere. People break down

in hospital corridors.
Train bridges collapse.
A desperate man burns down his own barn.

A wasp hugs a paralyzed cutworm.

A corn-poppy nods in a field
of unfocused grass.

Agate-coloured spheres circle noiselessly
among wakeful stars.

A professor walks through ruins
while cleaning his glasses.

A scowling officer with a patch over one eye
parts the slats of a blind.

Mysterious boxes are unloaded.

Flies settle on a child dying in a pile of garbage.

A young man explains how to wax skis.

Oh no, it is wasting my time!
I am forgetting to harvest the pumpkins,
the pumpkins are rotting in the field.
The animals haven't been fed.
I have forgotten to sleep
and am spending my night watching people I don't know
pretend to be people I don't know.
It isn't real.

But what did I ever get from being real?
You run a huge risk in the world —

If you walk there, you will die.
If you eat that, you will die.
If you stand under those, you will die.

But here in the shared light
I can die every minute
and stand up again, yawning and stretching.

Here, the future
is practised until it is perfect.
The past is preserved
until it is needed, and I,
I am killing time without mercy
to the sound of bodiless laughter
ghostly orchestras
and frantic applause.

American Fireworks in Montreal

A summer night, the cooked air
blackens like a fuse.
A double jet trail fades to black.
In the doorway, light is at my back,
coils of steam are rising from my hair.
My murderous neighbour spreads himself a snack
in his yellow kitchen. Everywhere,
music is leaking from the cracks
in peoples' lives, from windows, from car doors.
From my neighbour's house, a muffled war
on channel twelve.
I latch the window and fix tea
in the flickering blue light of his TV.

Tonight there are fireworks. On the quay
along the harbour, in the island park,
half the city gathers in the dark
to witness a controlled catastrophe.
I go too, so does the guy next door,
and half a million of us make our way
to the warehouse village
where a bridge named Jacques Cartier,
looms like a stupendous photostat
in the sky above the street,
stepping through homes on steel and granite feet,
big enough to stomp the city flat.

People are roosting in the trees.
They crouch in pylons. I see faces
in the punched-out windows of the factories.
The best spots are already gone.
We infiltrate a scrapyard on our knees
through broken places in a chain-link fence,
and there are hundreds of us scaling an immense
moraine of rusted tricycles and tools.
Around me, disembodied strangers shout

to other strangers. I can just make out
my neighbour's thin, machine-like silhouette
picking its way through wreckage
by the red light of his cigarette.

Darkness thickens over Notre Dame;
a little sunlight seeps
through bandages of cloud
on the bruised horizon. In the crowd
someone says to nobody, aloud,
in a peculiar voice: I don't know where I am.

And now the fireworks. Blam.
A parachute of violet fire
sinks to the river. Blam. A shower
of radioactive seaweed. Blam. Blam. Blam.
A bomb inside a ball in an exploding flower,
sketched against the fountains of Versailles,
with a welder's torch. Cinders fly
in shallow arches, whistling as they die
and trolling incandescent smoke. And then,
expanding and contracting worlds
beaten apart by comets, hurled
from a revolving nautilus; at last,
a kind of writhing Gorgon's-head of light,
scorched on our eyelids. Paralyzed with fright,
we scratch our heads and yawn.
In the darkness, someone shouts: Right on.
Someone answers: U.S.A., *alright*.

In half an hour everyone is gone,
and I'm gone too, paddling my bike through fog.
I lock it to my neighbour's iron grill
and climb upstairs.
The night is very still.
My neighbour's ugly, ladle-footed dog

is whimpering for my neighbour. I can hear it scrape
its animal fingers on the locked screen door.
I spread a blanket on the fire escape
and lie awake on it till four,
then fall asleep. I dream some war
has scrubbed the planet clean, and wake at five
in the blazing vacancy of dawn.
I am the only sentient thing alive
to breathe this freshness. Avalon.
The sky is white. Circles of white
birds hang like brushstrokes on the white
sky; a single jet trail, white,
dissolves to nothing in a wispy "S".
Nothing is emptier, or means less.
Nothing explains this light.

Doodle

I have doodled a fantastic picture,
definitely worth keeping.
But what does it mean?
It shows a man in black pajamas sleeping
in a black gelatinous machine.
He is a lunatic, I think.
He dreams of piloting a submarine
in latitudes of permanent black ink
through oceans of condensed malarkey,
spirals, hieroglyphics, grids,
corkscrews, checkerboards and pyramids.
But he is not himself at all.
His mind feels funny being fondled by
that Muse of Incoherence who reclines
above him on a cloud of wavy lines,
jumbling the objects in his sky.
Chinese letters and occult designs.
What could any of it signify?
That ink is shallow, and yet deep.
That meanings mate and multiply,
tousling the air above our sleep.
That q resembles p, as x does y.

Or something else. But what? The truth
Is tortuous, you'd be surprised.
This drowsy harlequin materialized
while I was on the telephone arranging
for a cheque I'd written not to bounce.
I had some funds transferred between accounts,
and as my ghostly treasures were exchanging
values in the hidden vaults
of the magnetic storage-chambers where
the ciphers of my hedonism waltz,
this thing began appearing in a corner
of a page of my agenda and
inexorably snuck across the paper,

self-engendered, eerily unplanned,
like Escher's famous drawing of a hand
that draws a hand that draws another hand.

It happens quietly, without commotion.
Your mind is elsewhere. Something interferes
with empty paper and a thing appears:
a madman on a jewelled ocean.
And that is what my poem wants as well,
to make things happen, but without exertion —
baffling arabesques unfurled
like faxes from the underworld
in one authoritative motion.

It needs the fluency and expertise
of the ingenious, brainless world,
which doodles on itself incessantly,
scribbling meanders on the parched plateaus,
Moroccan carpets on a reptile's back,
black veins in the pliations of a rose,
medieval riddles in a woodworm's track.
The world is lavish, never at a loss.
It puts a caterpillar in a ball of string,
then dresses it in oriental cloth —
batik for the monarch's wing,
paisley for the moth.

It does all that without a plan,
lacquering the beetle's shell,
kinking the horns of the gazelle,
composing tracts of timeless nonsense
in the cursive of the runner bean.
Does anyone who sits beneath a willow
know what its gesticulations mean?
The speechless bulk of the created world
is made entirely out of marginalia,

weird caprices that assail
the central tissues. Oh, to fill the pale
middle of my life with frail
finials and diaphanous rosettes
and have a heart as pink and ruffled
and confused as an azalea!

Moon Town

Life is short, but afternoons are long.
Adrift in the vastness of
a tuesday, I used to put my cheek
up to the perforated hardboard
behind the TV to feel its heat,
looking in at the red vitals
of our modernity, and I knew that we
were in training for a strange
future, for lives filled with
dial gauges and horseshoe magnets,
moon towns and mechanical pets.
And it has been strange,
but one thing has never changed, I still
look into the future
closely inspecting the days left,
staring at them until they grow transparent,
like the blades of a fan.

Acknowledgements

Some of these poems appeared in the magazines *Literary Review of Canada*, *The Fiddlehead*, *The New Quarterly*, *The Malahat Review*, *Saturday Night*, *Scrivener*, *Prism International*, *Four by Four*, *Rubicon*, and in the anthologies *Penned: Zoo Poems* (2010), *The New Canon* (2005), *Sounds New* (1989), and *Poets 88* (1988).

"Definitely Not" and "Pacific Coho" were originally commissioned for the CBC program *Definitely Not the Opera*. "Ephemeroptera" was written for the CBC program *Canada Reads*. "Getting Around to It" and parts of "Nature" were aired on the CBC programs *All in a Day* and *Ottawa Morning*. Thanks to Barbara Carey, assigner of tasks and reassuring voice in the earphones.

"Foreigners," "A Word I Dislike," "Camels nor Millionaires," "Viking Winter," "To my Body," "Petit Marcel," "Dionysian Revels," "Changes of Weather," and "Old Love Song" first appeared in the letterpress chapbook *Getting on with the Era* (Villeneuve, 1987). All but the first two were republished in *Cold Rubber Feet* (Cormorant, 1989). "Social Studies," "Shed," *"Les Souvenirs,"* "400 Jobs in Murdochville," and "Tackle" also appeared in *Cold Rubber Feet*.

The following poems are reprinted from *Facts* (Signal / Véhicule, 1999): "Doodle," "Tomato Hornworm," "March 1," "The Slough," "Moon Town," "Spring," "Idleness," "Lovely," *"Palais de Justice,"* "Orangutans," "American Fireworks," "TV," "My Son," "Spook," "Vocal Accompaniment," "Erythronium". Grateful thanks to Véhicule Press for permission to include them in this volume.

I would like to thank the editors of these earlier collections, Fred Louder and Robyn Sarah, Jan Geddes, and Michael Harris. Thanks as well to Carmine Starnino for generous inclusion of my work in *The New Canon*.

I am grateful to the Canada Council for the Arts for their generous support.

For Robyn Sarah, whose encouragement & good example made this book exist, "grateful acknowledgements" seem pretty stingy, but it's what this page is for. Thanks, then, but also affection and admiration, if those are permitted here. "We write on Time."

About the Author

Bruce Taylor was twice recipient of the A.M. Klein Award, for his earlier poetry collections *Cold Rubber Feet* (1987) and *Facts* (1998). More recently, his poems have appeared in *The New Quarterly*, *The Fiddlehead*, and *Literary Review of Canada*, and have been featured on CBC. He lives in Wakefield, Quebec, with his wife and three children.

Author photo: Maggie Odell.